I0799311

TABLE OF CONTENTS

This image shows Arsenal players in action during the 1906–1907 season.

SOCCER'S Greatest Clubs

Arsenal FC

Joel Newsome

Cavendish Square
New York

Published in 2021 by Cavendish Square Publishing, LLC
243 5th Avenue, Suite 136, New York, NY 10016

Copyright © 2021 by Cavendish Square Publishing, LLC

First Edition

No part of this publication may be reproduced, stored in a retrieval system, or transmitted in any form or by any means—electronic, mechanical, photocopying, recording, or otherwise—without the prior permission of the copyright owner. Request for permission should be addressed to Permissions, Cavendish Square Publishing, 243 5th Avenue, Suite 136, New York, NY 10016. Tel (877) 980-4450; fax (877) 980-4454.

Website: cavendishsq.com

This publication represents the opinions and views of the author based on his or her personal experience, knowledge, and research. The information in this book serves as a general guide only. The author and publisher have used their best efforts in preparing this book and disclaim liability rising directly or indirectly from the use and application of this book.

All websites were available and accurate when this book was sent to press.

Library of Congress Cataloging-in-Publication Data

Names: Newsome, Joel, author. | Cavendish Square Publishing LLC.
Title: Arsenal FC / Joel Newsome.
Other titles: Arsenal Football Club
Description: First Edition. | New York : Cavendish Square Publishing, 2021. | Series: Soccer's greatest clubs | Includes webography.
Identifiers: LCCN 2019047056 (print) | LCCN 2019047057 (ebook) | ISBN 9781502652836 (Library Binding) | ISBN 9781502652829 (Paperback) | ISBN 9781502652843 (eBook)
Subjects: LCSH: Arsenal Football Club.
Classification: LCC GV943.6.L6 N49 2021 (print) | LCC GV943.6.L6 (ebook) | DDC 796.334/630942143--dc23
LC record available at https://lccn.loc.gov/2019047056
LC ebook record available at https://lccn.loc.gov/2019047057

Editor: Kristen Susienka
Copy Editor: Rebecca Rohan
Designer: Joe Parenteau

The photographs in this book are used by permission and through the courtesy of: Cover Vlad1988/Shutterstock.com; series art (badge) Onur Cem/Shutterstock.com; series art (field) comzeal images/Shutterstock.com; series art (soccer ball) FocusStocker/Shutterstock.com; series art (crowd silhouette) Nosyrevy/Shutterstock.com; p. 4 Popperfoto via Getty Images/Getty Images; pp. 7, 12 Bob Thomas/Popperfoto via Getty Images/Getty Images; p. 9 Evening Standard/Hulton Archive/Getty Images; p. 11 (both) Bridgeman Images; p. 14 Topical Press Agency/Getty Images; p. 18 J. Gaiger/Topical Press Agency/Getty Images; p. 20 Keystone/Getty Images; pp. 23, 27 PA Images via Getty Images; p. 28 Clive Rose/Getty Images; p. 31 Shaun Botterill/Getty Images; p. 32 Alex Livesey/Getty Images; p. 36 Charlotte Wilson/Offside/Getty Images; p. 37 Clive Mason/Getty Images; p. 38 Clive Brunskill/Getty Images; pp. 40 Martin Rickett – PA Images/PA Images via Getty Images; pp. 41, 48 AMA/Corbis via Getty Images; p. 47 Alexander Scheuber – UEFA/UEFA via Getty Images; p. 50 Michael Regan/Getty Images; p. 52 Adam Davy/PA Images via Getty Images; p. 53 Bundit Sriusaneemorakot/Shutterstock.com; p. 54 Visionhaus/Getty Images Europe/Getty Images.

CPSIA compliance information: Batch #CS20CSQ: For further information contact Cavendish Square Publishing LLC, New York, New York, at 1-877-980-4450.

Printed in the United States of America

Find us on

1 WHO IS ARSENAL FC?

Arsenal Football Club (FC) is a professional English soccer team in London, England. It's one of the top teams in modern sports. In England and much of the rest of the world, soccer is called football, which is why the team name ends with "Football Club."

ORIGINS OF SOCCER

Soccer started as a combination between two sports: rugby football and association football. In England, where it first became popular, the two sports separated from each other in the 1860s. The modern version of soccer began. Soon, it became the most popular sport in Europe and much of the world.

Soccer is played on a field, called a pitch, with 11 players on each side. Two teams play each other on the pitch for two halves with a short break, or halftime, in between. Each half is 45 minutes long, for a total of 90 minutes per game. Each team wants to score the most points, or goals, in nets on opposite ends of the field. The team with the most points wins. Sometimes, there's a tie. Some games end in ties, but

SPORT SHORT

The year of Arsenal's start—1886—was the same year the United Kingdom's Hockey Association formed.

for very important games, the teams play for 30 more minutes. This is called extra time. If the score is still tied, the teams go to a shootout. A shootout is when a player kicks the ball at the net with only the goalkeeper standing in their way. Whichever team scores the most goals on penalty kicks (out of five chances) wins the game.

ARSENAL SITS AT THE TOP

Arsenal reached the top level of English soccer in 1904 and has only been relegated, or moved down to a lower level of soccer, once. This makes them the team with the longest streak of staying at the top level. Arsenal also has played the most games in a row without being beaten. The team plays its home games at Emirates Stadium in London, England, and has many dedicated fans.

Though Arsenal is one of the most successful soccer teams, its beginnings were decidedly humble.

DIAL SQUARE

In 1886, a group of coworkers at Woolwich Arsenal Armament Factory realized they had something in common: a shared enthusiasm for soccer. David Danskin was a Scottish engineer and amateur soccer player who moved to London in 1885 for work. There, he met fellow soccer fans Jack Humble, Elijah Watkins, and Richard Pearce. Three men who had played for a soccer team called Nottingham Forest—Fred Beardsley, Bill Parr and Charles Bates—joined them. These men recruited 15 others and worked together to buy a ball. Though they had a ball and enough players for a team, the group lacked a name. They also had no uniform and no home field to practice and play on.

Despite all of these missing parts, the team scheduled their first match—another word for a game—for December 11, 1886, against a team called Eastern Wanderers. The ragtag bunch of coworkers originally referred to themselves as Dial Square after

Shown here are early Arsenal players, who look a lot different from players today!

a workshop in the factory. Dial Square won the match 6–0. Two weeks later, the newly formed, undefeated team met in Royal Oak, a pub near Woolwich Arsenal Station, to celebrate their victory. During the festivities, the men decided to rename their promising new team by combining the name of their workplace with the name of the pub. They began referring to themselves as Royal Arsenal.

In an effort to solve the problem of not having a proper uniform, Fred Beardsley had reached out to his former team, Nottingham Forest, for help. They promptly sent Beardsley enough red shirts for each player. Since then, red has been Arsenal's main color on the field.

WOOLWICH ARSENAL

For the next five years, Royal Arsenal played games at a field called Plumstead Common. Plumstead was a park close to the Woolwich Arsenal factory. Soon, however, more and more of Plumstead Common's land was being used to build houses for Woolwich Arsenal's growing workforce, and the team decided to move to Manor Ground, a soccer stadium in southeast London. It lacked stands, or areas for fans to watch the games, and was located very close to a major sewer, which made the area smell. In 1890, Royal Arsenal moved again to Invicta Ground, a better stadium in southeast London. This area had stands and changing rooms. When Royal Arsenal relocated to Invicta Ground, they had a small following of about 1,000 fans.

Before long, they changed their name to Woolwich Arsenal. Soon after that, their fan group grew by the

This photograph shows an early Arsenal match.

thousands. Everyone wanted to see them play. On March 30, 1891, Woolwich Arsenal hosted Hearts of Midlothian, a Scottish soccer club, at Invicta Ground. Woolwich Arsenal lost the match 5–1 but managed to attract a record 12,000 spectators.

In 1893, Woolwich Arsenal officially joined the Second Division of the English Football League (EFL), making it the first team from the South of London to turn professional. The EFL is the main soccer organization in England.

Today, the English soccer system has four divisions. Teams of the same ability level are put into similar divisions, so the best teams are in the top division, or the Premier League, which isn't actually part of the EFL. Lesser teams play in the EFL divisions called the Championship League, League One, and League Two. The Championship League is the top EFL division.

Arsenal hoped to play its first EFL season at Invicta Ground, but George Weaver, the owner of Invicta Ground, had also noticed the team's growing success and raised the cost of rent. Instead of paying Weaver's price, the team decided to move back to Manor Ground. They bought the property and spent the summer of 1893 redesigning Manor Ground. They included stands and other elements appropriate for a sports venue.

On September 2, 1893, Woolwich Arsenal played their first match in the EFL against Newcastle United, another recent addition to the league. The match ended 2–2. A week later, their second match ended in defeat, with Notts County beating Woolwich Arsenal 3–2. They rallied days later when Joseph Heath scored the team's first hat trick (three goals in a game) against the Walsall Town Swifts, defeating them 4–0.

Though Arsenal had their fair share of losses that first season, they finished in 9th place out of 15 teams. One of their most impressive victories came against Ashford United on October 14, 1893. With a score of 12–0, the newly professional factory workers had won their biggest victory yet in a Footbal Association (FA) Cup match. The FA Cup is the Football Association group's top competition among the best teams in

SPORT SHORT

Arsenal has been known by many names, but the team's most popular nickname, the Gunners, refers to the Arsenal Armament Factory where the team's founders worked.

In the 1900s, Arsenal players were featured in cartoon drawings, like these of Tim Coleman and Jimmy Ashcroft from 1907.

the sport. The Football Association is another main governing soccer group in England.

Woolwich Arsenal chose Harry Bradshaw as their manager, or head coach, in 1899. Bradshaw had formerly managed Burnley, another team in the EFL. Bradshaw had been able to improve Burnley enough to move them from the EFL's Second Division, or second level, to the First Division, or top level. In fact, in his last season with Burnley, they finished third in their division, which was their best ranking in the team's history.

ARSENAL'S CHANGING UNIFORM

Former Nottingham Forest players found a way to outfit the newly created Woolwich Arsenal by asking old teammates for old uniforms. While Arsenal's jersey was at first determined by opportunity, it inspired other teams to play in red. In fact, the Czech soccer club Sparta Prague wears red because their former president saw Woolwich Arsenal play in London in 1906. He was so impressed with the uniforms that he chose the same colors for his team.

Manager Herbert Chapman introduced a key change to Arsenal's look in 1925. He decided to add a white collar and sleeves to the red shirts. These uniforms were the first to show the club badge, which was positioned on the left side. The cannon that often symbolizes the team didn't appear until 1967. Updates to the style of the team's jerseys continue today, usually because a sponsor changes or a different company makes the uniform. Both sponsor and uniform designer names are on each jersey.

The white collars of Arsenal's uniform can be seen in this photo of the team from before the 1932 FA Cup Final.

When Bradshaw joined Woolwich Arsenal, he immediately brought in several new players. He signed Jimmy Ashcroft, a talented goalkeeper; Jimmy Jackson, who would become the team captain, or lead player; and Percy Sands, who would go on to spend 17 years with the club. Bradshaw was influenced by Scottish soccer and emphasized short passing along with easy and almost unnoticeable movement into positions on the field. With Bradshaw's guidance, Woolwich Arsenal was able to improve enough to finish second in the 1903–1904 season. With that, the club was promoted to the First Division. Altogether, Woolwich Arsenal played 11 seasons in the Second Division. By the time the club reached the First Division, Bradshaw had brought in 18 of their 20 players.

Shown here are Arsenal and Newcastle United captains before a match in 1919.

2 ARSENAL'S CONTINUING HISTORY

In May 1904, Harry Bradshaw left Arsenal to manage Fulham, another English soccer team. With Bradshaw gone, Woolwich Arsenal struggled in the First Division. They reached the semifinals in 1905–1906 and in 1906–1907, but they only managed to finish better than 10th place twice between 1904 and 1913.

MONEY MANAGEMENT

During this time, lack of money played a big part in Arsenal's troubles. The club was on the edge of London at the time. This meant not many people wanted to travel there to watch games. Low game attendance meant the team wasn't making a lot of money. To make money, the club had to move some of their best players to other teams. In soccer, this is known as "selling" today. However, without their best players, the team didn't play very well. This also hurt the team's fans. Not many wanted to watch games if the team didn't win. By 1910, attendance fell to almost half of what it had been in 1904. It was clear some kind of change needed to happen.

In 1910, the club was purchased by a group of businessmen. One of them was Henry Norris, a politician who was also the chairman, or president, of the Fulham soccer team. Norris knew that big changes were necessary to save Arsenal. At first, he tried to join Woolwich Arsenal with Fulham, but the EFL would only agree if the new, combined team joined the Second Division. Norris had wanted the team to take Arsenal's place in the First Division, so no new team was created. Norris then had the idea to move the club to another location. After careful consideration, he chose an area called Highbury, in North London.

Though local fans and Highbury residents didn't like the idea at first, a new stadium was eventually built. The team moved there at the end of the 1912–1913 season, in which they finished last. Because of that, they were moved to the Second Division. Though their play had suffered, Woolwich Arsenal's fortune began to turn because their new location brought in more fans. Their first season at Highbury drew average crowds of about 23,000.

In April 1914, the club decided to drop Woolwich from their name and became known as "The Arsenal." The 1914–1915 season was played as World War I began to spread aound the globe, and The Arsenal finished in sixth place. During the war, many players went to fight.

SPORT SHORT

On January 22, 1927, Arsenal's match against Sheffield United was the first English League match to be aired on a live radio broadcast.

Some didn't return. However, The Arsenal continued playing after the fighting ended.

In 1919, the club was desperate to be back in the First Division. New rules to the league also meant there were 22 teams rather than 20 for the first time in the First Division. The Arsenal didn't have a great standing in the Second Division (they were fifth), but it was argued that they should be promoted because of their history of service to the league. Even though there were teams with better records that had been in the league longer, the league agreed and sent The Arsenal back to the First Division in 1919.

By the end of 1919, the club began dropping "The" from its name and slowly began referring to themselves simply as Arsenal. Today, most people around the world know the team by that name.

While Arsenal managed to find its way back into the First Division, the team continued to struggle. Norris made Leslie Knighton manager, and during his time with the team, Arsenal never finished better than ninth place. In fact, they came close to being relegated to the Second Division once again by finishing 19th in the 1923–1924 season and 20th in the 1924–1925 season. Norris fired Knighton in May 1925 and hired Herbert Chapman, a former player and manager who had helped Huddersfield Town win the FA Cup and two First Division titles in four years. Norris hoped Chapman could help Arsenal have similar success.

THE BANK OF ENGLAND CLUB

Herbert Chapman set about rebuilding Arsenal. He hired Tom Whittaker as team trainer and signed player

Iconic Arsenal coach Herbert Chapman (*center*) is shown here with Alex James (*right*), one of his most dynamic players, before the 1932 FA Cup final.

Charles Buchan, a veteran from Sunderland. Buchan's influence included more than his experience in playing the game. He worked with Whittaker and Chapman to adopt a player formation on the pitch that helped Arsenal's defense. Arsenal finished second in the league in Chapman's first season. In the following years, their performance dipped again, but the new manager had faith that things would turn around and continued to make changes.

Chapman signed players David Jack, Alex James, Cliff Bastin, and Eddie Hapgood and made sure players were paid well. By 1930, Chapman's improvements were starting to work. That year, Arsenal won the FA Cup final against Chapman's old team, Huddersfield Town. The club went on to win the First Division in the 1930–1931 season and then again in 1932–1933.

Chapman's additions to Arsenal helped the team grow. As they began having success on the field, they brought in record-breaking crowds. Star players were earning top salaries, so people began referring to Arsenal as "the Bank of England Club." This was a comment that meant the team was making a lot of money.

However, tragedy struck at the beginning of the 1933–1934 season when Herbert Chapman died suddenly from pneumonia. The club was mourning his loss when Joe Shaw took over until that summer. George Allison became manager after him. Under the guidance of Shaw and Allison, Arsenal won league titles in 1933–1934, 1934–1935, and 1937–1938. In 1934, seven Arsenal players were chosen to play on the English World Cup team. Arsenal also won the FA Cup in 1936. The outbreak of World War II in 1939 meant a pause in British soccer, but by then, Arsenal was a top team.

POSTWAR PLAY

The start of World War II meant a seven-year stop to soccer playing in England. Competitive play continued in 1946, after the end of the war, and Arsenal struggled

During World War II, members of Arsenal traveled to Germany to play against service teams as entertainment for the troops.

in their first postwar season. The team ended in 13th place, their worst ranking in 17 years. George Allison retired, and Tom Whittaker took his place as manager. In 1947–1948, Arsenal won the league title. Whittaker added some younger players. In the 1949–1950 season, the slightly younger Arsenal team beat Liverpool 2–0 to win the FA Cup. The 1952–1953 season gave Arsenal its seventh league title, but it was the last trophy the club earned for almost 20 years.

STRUGGLES

The years that followed Arsenal's seventh league title were hard on the team. Players were aging, and Arsenal struggled to attract younger players. The sudden death of Tom Whittaker in 1956 only worsened matters. The club stumbled through the 1950s and

1960, though there were some high points. They finished fifth in 1955–1956 and 1956–1957 and took third place in 1958–1959. Billy Wright, a former player for the Wolverhampton Wanderers, became manager in 1962, and while his efforts didn't return Arsenal to its former glory, they did mean the team finished seventh in 1962–1963. This ranking was good enough to qualify the club for the Inter-Cities Fairs Cup, their first wider European contest.

Wright was replaced by Bertie Mee in 1966. Mee's appointment was met with uncertainty by many, including Mee himself. It's said Mee asked for a line in his contract to state that he could return to his former position as the team's physiotherapist if the manager role didn't suit him. However, history would see Mee greatly improve the team.

THE FIRST DOUBLE

Mee focused on promoting players from Arsenal's youth team, the team of players under the age of 21 that the club trained in the hope that they could play for Arsenal's top team one day. This approach seemed to work. Arsenal reached the League Cup finals in 1968 and 1969, though they were defeated both years. Even so, Arsenal finished fourth in 1969, making them able to compete in Europe for the 1970 Inter-Cities Fairs Cup. The team got the win, and their first European title, by defeating Belgian team Anderlecht 4–3. In the 1970–1971 season, Arsenal became the second team in the 20th century to win the coveted Double. This meant the team won the league's top spot and the FA Cup.

SEVENTIES SLUMP

The 1971–1972 season didn't start well for Arsenal, and they ended up finishing fifth. The next season, Arsenal managed a second-place finish in the First Division, but their performance fell sharply in subsequent seasons. The club came in 16th and 17th in 1974–1975 and 1975–1976, forcing Mee to leave.

A man named Terry Neill took over. Neill had managed English team Tottenham and had played for Arsenal. He was also the team's youngest manager at that time. Neill led Arsenal to three FA Cup finals, in 1978, 1979, and 1980. The club had a famous FA Cup victory in 1979 against Manchester United but was defeated in 1978 and 1980.

Neill's success was due in part to several very talented Irish players on the team. The most influential was Liam Brady. However, Brady left the team in the summer of 1980, starting yet another season of few highlights for the Gunners. While they stayed in the top four spots of the First Division in the early 1980s, Arsenal failed to make a serious run for the FA Cup. Neill was fired in 1983, and the club struggled to find a worthy replacement. It would take another former Gunner to turn the team around.

GRAHAM'S GAME

In 1986, George Graham became manager of Arsenal and turned his attention to bringing success back to the club. Graham had played for Arsenal during their first Double victory, when Bertie Mee was manager. As a result, he knew what a winning team looked like and

THE NORTH LONDON RIVALRY

Shown here is a match between Tottenham Hotspur and Arsenal—two historic rivals.

In soccer, local teams often have rivalries. The games played between these teams are called derbies. The rivalry between Arsenal and Tottenham Hotspur is referred to as the North London derby. Their competition started in 1919 when Arsenal was promoted to the First Division. Tottenham had been relegated that same season, but if Arsenal hadn't been allowed in the First Division, Tottenham would've taken their spot.

Over the years, Arsenal has often defeated the Spurs, as Tottenham is called. The two teams have met almost 200 times and Tottenham has won less than 60 of those matches. The historic snub and shared geographical area have made the Spurs' struggle to emerge from Arsenal's shadow nearly unbearable for Tottenham fans.

SPORT SHORT

The 1939 film *The Arsenal Stadium Mystery* featured several Arsenal players and staff and was one of the first films to use soccer as a key plot element.

how it should work. Graham promoted talented players from the youth team while also signing new talent and gradually moving older players to other teams. He was much stricter than former managers, and his influence was immediately apparent. By Christmas 1986, Arsenal was at the top of the First Division. The Gunners ended up finishing fourth in the 1986–1987 season but they also won their first League Cup. The following season, Arsenal had the sixth-best record and reached the finals in the League Cup. However, they fell to Luton Town. Though the team's performance had slipped slightly, Graham had revamped the defense with players Nigel Winterburn, Lee Dixon, and Steve Bould. These players, along with Tony Adams, formed the famous "Back Four," a unit that opposing offenses found nearly impossible to beat.

100 YEARS OF FOOTBALL

In April 1988, the league put together a celebratory tournament to mark 100 years of English soccer. It was called the Football League Centenary Trophy. It was a knockout competition (a competition in which only winning teams move forward each round) between the top eight teams in the First Division. Arsenal ranked sixth that season and made it to the competition. They easily defeated Queens Park Rangers in the quarterfinals. In the semifinals, Arsenal faced Liverpool and beat them 2–1. The Gunners moved into the finals, where they faced Manchester United for the trophy. On October 9, 1988, the two teams battled at Villa Park, the birthplace of the English Football League. In the end, the defense of the famous Back Four gave Arsenal the win.

CONTINUED SUCCESS AND CORRUPTION

Arsenal's thrilling triumph was followed with an even more exciting win during the 1988–1989 season. The league's title race was gripping that year, as several teams were in contention. In the end, it came down to Arsenal versus Liverpool, which was dealing with the aftermath of the Hillsborough disaster, a sporting accident where 96 soccer fans were crushed to death in Hillsborough Stadium before a match between Liverpool and Nottingham Forest on April 15, 1989.

Liverpool needed a tie with second-ranked Arsenal to secure the league title. Arsenal, however, needed to win by two goals to get the top spot. In the game, Arsenal's defense worked hard, eventually leaving Liverpool scoreless. A second and final goal in the last seconds from Arsenal's midfielder Michael Thomas meant Arsenal had won.

The 1990–1991 season saw Arsenal take the league title once again as they lost only one match. They dominated during the 1992–1993 season as well, winning both the FA Cup and the League Cup Double. In May 1994, they won the European Cup Winners' Cup and seemed unstoppable.

Unfortunately, it was found that Graham took an illegal bribe from Norwegian soccer agent Rune Hauge, who represented player John Jensen during his 1992 transfer to Arsenal. Graham was fired from the club and banned from the Football Association for one year as punishment. His replacement, Bruce Rioch, managed Arsenal during the 1995–1996 season but left after a dispute with the board of directors over the use of transfer funds. Though it seemed like the Gunners had fallen on tough times in terms of leadership, they would soon acquire the most successful manager in the history of the club: Arsène Wenger.

ARSENAL'S LONGEST MANAGER

Though Arsenal had seen much of its success come under the management of former players, the most successful Gunners' manager was a Frenchman who was relatively unknown to England when he took over. Arsène Wenger had managed teams in Austria, France, Italy, and Japan before joining Arsenal. While he was with the club, Arsenal dominated the league. Altogether, Wenger managed them for 22 years. Of the 1,228 games that Arsenal played under Wenger, they lost only 245. A whopping 704 ended in victory, with another 279 ending in a tie. The team scored 2,285 points while he was manager, while only 1,219 were scored on them. Seven of Arsenal's FA Cup titles were earned with Wenger leading the team.

Arsène Wenger became one of Arsenal's top coaches. Shown here is Wenger receiving a special award in 2003.

Arsenal players celebrate their 4–0 shutout win against Ashton Villa after the 2015 FA Cup final.

3 MORE MODERN SUCCESSES

When the new manager of Arsenal FC was announced in 1996, fans might not have expected to hear a name so similar to their team. As the headline of the *London Evening Standard* newspaper read, the thought on many people's minds was something like: "Arsène who?" Wenger was not a well-known figure in English soccer, but he had experience in other countries. His time with the team would signal a new era of Arsenal. Today, the team is highly successful thanks to him.

WENGER'S WAYS

Wenger made many changes to improve the team. He advised them on everything from what to eat to what types of exercises to do. For example, he brought in French fitness experts to explain how a diet of steamed fish, boiled chicken, and vegetables could energize them. On the practice field, Wenger had many opinions about training exercises. He wanted the players to do more plyometric movements, like skipping and jumping. These exercises stressed the joints but allowed players

SPORT SHORT

The Arsenal player with the most goals in a single match as of late 2019 is Ted Drake. He managed to score seven times in a game against Aston Villa in 1935.

to become stronger and faster quickly. Wenger ran grueling practices with a stopwatch. Intense sessions that typically lasted 45 minutes or less mimicked the effort players would put into games. On game day, Arsenal saw immediate results. In Wenger's first season at the helm, they finished third in the league. That success has only continued. Today, Arsenal is one of the strongest teams in the EFL.

Before Wenger's arrival, Arsenal had won the EFL Cup, known simply as the League Cup. Their first win came in 1987 and their second in 1993. Under Wenger, they came close but couldn't claim the top spot. The Gunners were runners-up in 2007, 2011, and 2018.

In other competitions, Arsenal has had more success. One of Arsenal's major moments came with a win in the 1994 Union of European Football Associations (UEFA) Cup Winners' Cup. This competition was between top European teams. Arsenal faced Parma, an Italian team, in the final. They won 1–0.

THE DOUBLE

To win a country's top division as well as the major cup competition in the same season is tough but rewarding. Wenger's Arsenal team clinched the Double twice, in 1997–1998 and 2001–2002. The 1997–1998 Double marked the first time a foreign-born manager's team had won it. Wenger was named that year's Premier League Manager of the Season in recognition of his accomplishment. The Premier League was a new level of soccer created in 1992. It was one level above the EFL's top division.

The Gunners won the league in 2001–2002 by seven points. They faced Chelsea in the FA Cup final. Midfielder Raymond Parlour scored first after 70 minutes of play. Just after Parlour received the ball from winger Claude Wiltord, sports journalist Tim Lovejoy reassured his audience, "Oh, it's all right. It's only Ray Parlour." As if on cue, Parlour shot the ball and landed the match's first goal in the upper-right corner of the net. Freddie Ljungberg added to Arsenal's lead 10 minutes later with a curling shot that sealed the win.

Arsenal players celebrate winning the FA Cup in 2002.

THE GOLDEN BOOT

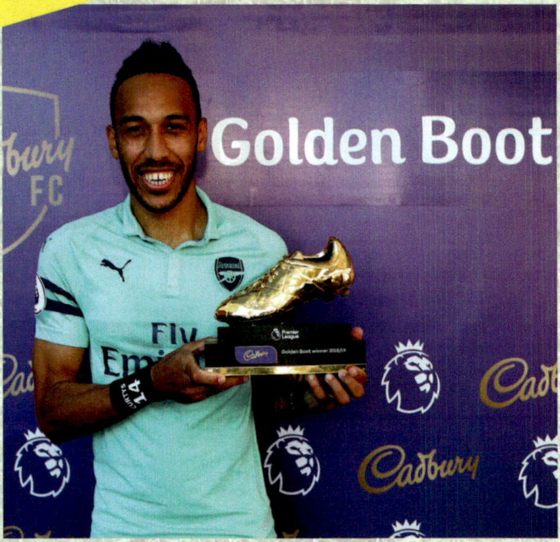

Arsenal's Pierre-Emerick Aubameyang won the Premier League's Golden Boot award during the 2018–2019 season.

One of the highest honors in professional soccer is the Golden Boot, a tribute awarded to the player(s) with the most goals scored in a league. The Premier League and European League both give a Golden Boot award to the highest scorer in their leagues. Arsenal's exceptional striker Thierry Henry received the European League Golden Boot in 2004 and 2005. He won the Premier League honor in 2004 and 2005 and added a third consecutive Premier League statue in 2006. In 2012, forward Robin van Persie earned the Premiere League golden boot with Arsenal and won again the following season after transferring to Manchester United. In 2019, three players from different teams earned the award in the Premier League. Liverpool's winger Sadio Mané and their forward Mohamed Salah, as well as Arsenal's striker Pierre-Emerick Aubameyang, all scored 22 goals, tying for most in the league.

The second Double in four years earned Wenger the Premier League Manager of the Season Award along with the BBC Sport Personality of the Year Coach Award for 2001–2002.

FA CUPS

The Gunners have lifted the FA Cup 13 times in their history as of late 2019, the most of any club. Perhaps more impressive is the fact that the majority of these victories came under the management of Arsène Wenger. The Frenchman secured seven FA Cups while managing Arsenal.

The 1997–1998 season was Wenger's second with the team, and the FA Cup final was momentous in that they were facing Newcastle United. Both teams had won the cup six times at that point. It was also the third time they had faced each other in the final—with Newcastle the victors twice before. Arsenal was playing for their new manager, for glory, and for redemption. With goals from winger Marc Overmars and Nicolas Anelka, Arsenal's defense took care of the rest. The match ended 2–0, with Arsenal the winner.

In 2002, Arsenal faced Chelsea for the FA Cup. Arsenal's defense was once again on full display that day, and the match ended 2–0 in favor of the Gunners.

The 2003 FA Cup was the first to be played indoors because of bad weather. Arsenal faced off against Southampton. The winning goal was landed late in the first half. Freddie Ljungberg's attempt was blocked, but the ball was quickly recovered by the Gunners, and Robert Pires was able to land the goal. The defense held off Southampton, and Arsenal retained the trophy for the second year in a row.

The 2005 FA Cup final saw Arsenal take on Manchester United. The match was intensely competitive. Neither team scored in the first 90 minutes of play nor in the 30 minutes of extra time. The game was decided by a shootout, the first in FA Cup history. Manchester United's Ruud Van Nistelrooy took the first shot and sunk the ball high into the net as Arsenal goalkeeper Jens Lehmann dove to the left. Lauren, Arsenal's right back, took the next shot and evened the score 1–1. Paul Scholes was next up for Manchester United, and this time, Lehmann dove into the path of the ball and prevented another point being scored. Both teams scored three times on the following six attempts. For Arsenal, Ljungberg sailed the ball into the middle of the goal, forward Robin van Persie curled the ball hard into the top right, and left back Ashley Cole popped the ball high into the net. Manchester United's shots landed as well, leaving Arsenal's Patrick Vieira with the final, potentially game-winning attempt. He kicked the ball toward the top left corner of the goal, and goalkeeper Roy Carroll dove toward it. However, it remained just out of his reach, giving Arsenal the win and their 10th FA Cup victory. They wouldn't taste FA Cup victory again for another nine years.

In 2014, Arsenal reached the FA Cup final once again and played against Hull City for the trophy. Another thriller, this match was competitive and high scoring. Sixteen minutes in, Arsenal scored their first goal with a penalty kick from right winger Santi Cazorla. Hull City led at the half with a score of 2–1. In the second half,

Arsenal struggled to tie things up and finally did in the 71st minute. At the end of 90 minutes, the game went into extra time. Arsenal came out aggressively. They scored with Aaron Ramsey firing a low shot past Hull City goalkeeper Allan McGregor. Both teams made additional attempts during the remaining extra time, but nothing landed, and the contest ended with a score of 3–2 and Arsenal taking the trophy.

In 2015, Arsenal returned to the FA Cup final. This time they faced Aston Villa, a team they had faced twice in the regular season. The FA Cup saw Arsenal dominating play with four goals against Aston Villa, which was unable to respond. In the end, a score of 4–0 made Arsenal the decided victors. The win gave Arsenal their 12th FA Cup, the most of any club at that point in history.

In 2017, the Gunners won their third FA Cup in four seasons with a 2–1 victory over Chelsea. The coverage leading up to the match highlighted the fact that it was essentially a rematch of the 2002 FA Cup final that saw Arsenal succeed over Chelsea 2–0.

Arsenal started fast and strong with a goal from Alex Sánchez four minutes in. The score remained 1–0 to Arsenal until Chelsea's Diego Costa evened things up with a goal in the 76th minute. The tied score lasted only three minutes, however. With a little over

SPORT SHORT

As of 2019, the highest-scoring Arsenal player in history is Thierry Henry, with a total of 228 goals for the Gunners.

ARSENAL WOMEN

Arsenal Women's Football Club celebrates a goal against Manchester City in 2018.

While Arsenal's professional men's team record is impressive, another Arsenal team's achievements are even more awe-inspiring. Women's soccer has been a part of Arsenal since 1987, when former player Vic Akers started a team. He went on to manage Arsenal Women for 22 years. Over that time, the team won 33 major titles, setting an incredible standard for women's English soccer. Included in this short but successful history is a season during which Arsenal Women won every league game and scored 119 goals while allowing only 10! They also won their league seven times in a row from 2003–2004 to the 2009–2010 season, six of which were unbeaten campaigns. Joe Montemurro took over as head coach in 2017. So far, during Montemurro's tenure, the team has won an FA Women's Super League championship and a Toulouse International Ladies Cup.

10 minutes left in regulation, Aaron Ramsey thrilled the crowd with a head shot past Chelsea goalkeeper Thibaut Courtois.

THE INVINCIBLES

Though Arsenal's glories are numerous, some might argue their greatest achievement came during the 2003–2004 season when the team went undefeated for 49 games. The Premier League commissioned a special trophy to honor the team's accomplishment. It was known as the Golden Trophy. In May 2018, Arsenal gifted the unique trophy to Arsène Wenger during their final home game under his management.

After his last home match as Arsenal's manager, Wenger hoisted his golden Premier League trophy, commemorating the unbeaten run of "The Invincibles," which is a nickname for the 2003–2004 team.

Marouane Fellaini of Manchester United (*above*) and Shkodran Mustafi of Arsenal (*below*) battle for control during a match in 2018.

4

CHALLENGES FOR THE TEAM

Even though Arsenal has had much success, the club has also faced challenges. More modern concerns have included financial, disciplinary, and athletic difficulties. No matter the problem, though, Arsenal has become stronger by working through them.

FINANCIAL CHALLENGES

As in other industries, professional sports teams need to spend money in order to make money. They do this by adding new players, building or improving stadiums, and making special clothing or other merchandise to sell to their fans. Sponsors are also important. A successful business often needs to balance these many parts. Arsène Wenger had a degree in economics. This made him useful in deciding where to use club funds. He also brought on a number of Arsenal players who breathed new life into the squad, and in his final years with Arsenal, he continued to do just that. However, some restructuring that began under Wenger has caused financial complications for the club in recent times.

In 2004, Arsenal was building a new stadium. It was to be completed in 2006 and named the Emirates Stadium, in honor of the airplane company that sponsored Arsenal. Financing for Emirates meant making careful decisions, especially about which players the club could afford to recruit. Arsenal missed out on acquiring soccer superstar Cristiano Ronaldo in 2003 because they couldn't afford to match Manchester United's offer of £12 million (just over $15 million). Wenger has said this is one of his biggest regrets during his time with the team. The signing of Alexandre Lacazette in 2017 cost the club £47 million

Cristiano Ronaldo (*in red*) is shown here in a game against Arsenal during his time with Manchester United.

SPORT SHORT

The Arsenal Clock was first located at Highbury Stadium. In 2006, it was relocated outside Emirates Stadium. A few years later, another, larger clock was placed inside the stadium to honor the team's history.

(over $57 million). Henrikh Mkhitaryan and Pierre-Emerick Aubameyang's contracts coupled with Wenger's exit set the club back even further financially. Wenger left a year before his contract officially ended, and Arsenal's board of directors agreed to pay him £11 million (over $13 million) as part of his leaving package.

One way to help bring in more money to a club is by getting more sponsors. Arsenal announced in May 2018 that they had signed a three-year partnership with the Rwanda Development Board. The agreement meant a "Visit Rwanda" patch would appear on the team's 2018–2019 uniform in exchange for money for the Gunners. The deal wasn't liked by everyone, though. Dutch authorities criticized Arsenal's contract because Rwanda receives aid from the Netherlands.

DISCIPLINARY ISSUES

Like all professional sports organizations, Arsenal teams have had their share of issues concerning players. From rambunctious behavior off the field to impassioned scrapping during and after competition, the Gunners

ARSENAL FINANCES

Arsenal has historically been one of the richest professional soccer clubs. However, their position has slipped in the 21st century. Deloitte Football Money League is an annual ranking of clubs based on how much money comes from soccer operations during the previous season. The most current rankings as of late 2019 saw Arsenal drop three positions, to ninth. Though some fans are nervous about the drop in rankings, Arsenal has several partnerships and sponsors that will help boost their brand and bring money to the club. Recently, the team agreed to partner with Adidas, which will design a new uniform for Arsenal. Technology companies like Acronis and Intel are also partnering with Arsenal. As a result, data science from practice sessions and matches are helping to highlight areas where players can improve. New 360-degree cameras will allow coaches, fans, and broadcasters to view matches from any angle, including player points of view. Arsenal is confident these partnerships will help players improve their performance on the pitch and also help the club get more money.

have navigated a variety of conduct challenges over the years.

BATTLE OF THE BUFFET

One of the most well-known modern conflicts involving Arsenal players happened in 2004. The Gunners were dominating their competition at the height of their season. On October 24, 2004, they faced Manchester United at Old Trafford, Manchester United's home stadium. Tensions ran high that day. The last nine Premier League titles had been claimed by either Arsenal or Manchester United. There was also bad blood between the teams; an interaction from the previous season still left a bad taste in the mouths of many. That match had been called the Battle at Old Trafford. In the coverage leading up to the 2004 match, the media referred to it as Battle at Old Trafford II.

Arsenal entered the match at the top of the Premier League, while Manchester United sat in sixth place, safely behind their competitors. The talk leading up to the match was ruthless. Sir Alex Ferguson, manager of Manchester United, told media outlets that Arsenal had the worst behavior he'd seen in the sport. Arsène Wenger brushed him off to the press, saying, "I hope that he will calm down." Manchester United was fueled by the opportunity for a redemptive rematch and the desire to stop Arsenal from getting 50 wins on their turf. The match was brutal, with many fouls throughout. Crucial calls were made in Manchester United's favor, the most consequential of which occurred 73 minutes into the match. Mike Riley, the referee, awarded a penalty to Manchester United after Arsenal's Sol Campbell and Manchester United's Wayne Rooney made contact.

Ruud Van Nistelrooy took the kick for Manchester United. Lehmann, Arsenal's goalkeeper, misjudged the ball's direction. Manchester United was up 1–0. Rooney scored the second goal during stoppage time. The score was 2–0 in favor of Manchester United. Arsenal's win streak had come to a close.

As the teams headed toward the players' tunnel, tensions boiled over. Wenger approached Van Nistelrooy about a play involving Arsenal's Ashley Cole. Ferguson stepped in and told Wenger to back off. The teams shouted at and jostled each other. Then, out of nowhere, pizza hit Ferguson in the face, and suddenly everyone stopped. Ferguson stomped off to the dressing room. When news of the scuffle reached the press, they dubbed the match "Battle of the Buffet." Wenger was fined for the confrontation, and Van Nistelrooy was disciplined for the foul on Cole. Both teams were required to meet with the Football Association. In 2017, Arsenal midfielder Cesc Fàbregas admitted to throwing the pizza.

RACISM

As in other parts of society, racism has appeared in professional soccer. This often involves fans shouting offensive words or phrases at players or other fans during games. Different international soccer groups have tried to address this issue. Players have too. One example is legendary Arsenal star Thierry Henry. He has been speaking out against racism in professional soccer for years. In 2019, he joined with Prince William on a British Broadcasting Company (BBC) documentary called *Royal Team Talk*, which featured discussions on men's mental health. Henry talked about some of his experiences with racism by fans while playing for Arsenal. Non-Arsenal players also face racism. Wilfried Zaha was insulted in person and on Twitter after Crystal Palace FC played Arsenal at Emirates Stadium in 2018.

In the 21st century, Arsenal has launched several investigations into abuse of players and other fans. The issue affects the entire international soccer-playing community. Several organizations are devoted to confronting racism, including Kick It Out and Show Racism the Red Card. Arsenal has partnered with these projects.

RED CARDS

Arsenal has also struggled with bad behavior on the field. Unai Emery, who took over the head coaching job after Wenger left, likes to see lots of attacking on the field. However, sometimes the players take this too far. Arsenal was set to finish within the top four teams on the Premier League table during the end of the 2018–2019 season, but three players received red cards over six matches. Red cards are given for bad behavior on the field. Sometimes, this means being too aggressive. After a team gets a red card, they have to play with one less player on the field. Getting so many red cards hurt Arsenal's playing. They managed to finish 2018–2019 in fifth place, but their performance left fans upset.

No matter what, problems are a part of life in professional sports. It's up to the players and the coaches to decide how to solve the problems on the field, and the soccer club and fan groups to decide how to solve problems off it.

ARSENAL'S MODERN RIVALS

While Arsenal's rivalry with fellow North London club Tottenham Hotspur has been around for decades, the Gunners' fiercest modern rivalries are with Manchester United and Chelsea.

Manchester United and Arsenal clashed most intensely in the 2000s. Manchester United was able to spoil Arsenal's win streak during the Invincibles era—the 2003–2004 season, where they went unbeaten in their 38 league matches, winning 26 games and earning a draw in 12. The two teams have a reputation for getting scrappy with each other, especially toward the end of matches. In 2019, Arsenal hosted Manchester United during the FA Cup. Manchester United won, but a fight broke out in the stands. Players from both sides shoved each other, and objects were thrown onto the field.

Chelsea won the league in 2005 and 2006, pulling the spotlight from Arsenal and Manchester United. While Chelsea and Arsenal have been competing together since 1907, they have only fought for major titles a few times. Chelsea's most crushing modern blow to Arsenal fans may have come in 2019 when Chelsea topped Arsenal in the UEFA Europa League final 4–1.

Olivier Giroud of Chelsea (*in the air, right*) battles Laurent Koscielny (*in the air, left*) of Arsenal for a header during the UEFA Europa League final on May 29, 2019.

Statues outside Emirates Stadium, such as this one of former coach Herbert Chapman, honor Arsenal's history.

5 ARSENAL'S FUTURE

As Arsenal approaches 150 years of being a soccer team, there is no question that the club has helped shape professional soccer. Starting as a new team in London in 1886, the Gunners are now one of the most popular teams in the world. It's exciting to think about where the team will go in the years ahead.

A NEW ERA

In 2018, after more than two decades, Arsène Wenger announced he was leaving the club. His reasons for leaving were mysterious, but many thought it was because Arsenal wasn't performing well in the 2018–2019 season. Fans were disappointed but also hopeful new manager Unai Emery would lead the team back to the top of the league.

A former soccer player, Emery had managed the French team Paris Saint-Germain from 2016 until 2018. Before that, he managed the Spanish team Sevilla. Under Emery's leadership, Sevilla won the Europa League (a European competition) three years in a row, making Emery one of only two managers to achieve this milestone.

In his first press conference after becoming Arsenal's head coach, Emery said, "My idea is to be protagonists all match … I want a squad [team] that is very, very intensive. It's two things that, for me, are very important." It seems Emery wants Arsenal to attack and pressure the other team at all times. This approach can lead to wins but also punishments for being too aggressive.

Arsenal lost their first two matches with Emery as head coach. However, they won their third and then went on to win the next 11 games. In fact, they managed to go unbeaten for 22 games. However, with a loss to Southampton, the team's luck ran out. Arsenal lost 10 more matches before playing in the Europa League final. Winning the competition could

In May 2018, Unai Emery joined Arsenal's coaching staff as manager, or team coach. Here he is in December 2018, during a game between Arsenal and Manchester United.

SPORT SHORT

In 2018, Arsenal announced an innovative 3MW battery system would be used to power Emirates Stadium during matches.

help Emery's reputation and set the tone for his time with the club. Though the new head coach had enjoyed victory with Sevilla, his work with Arsenal didn't lead to a win. They lost 4–1 to their rivals, Chelsea.

YOUTH TEAMS

Another way Arsenal is trying to improve is by having talented young players on their youth teams. Throughout the years, many players have joined the professional team from Arsenal's youth teams. In London, a special training center has been made to train young players. It's called the Arsenal Academy.

Today, promising young players include Arthur Okonkwo and Folarin Balogun. Mattéo Guendouzi, a young player from France, joined Arsenal's professional team from French team Lorient in 2018. Younger players have fresh skills to offer top teams, including Arsenal. Also, many players end their professional careers in their 30s, so keeping the future of the team in mind is always important. It's good to put the future in the hands of young people already dedicated to the team.

A NEW OWNER

In 2018, American billionaire Stan Kroenke became Arsenal's largest shareholder. This means he has full control of the business. He summed up his goal for

Arsène Wenger (*in white shirt*) and Arsenal owner Stan Kroenke can be seen here shaking hands.

Arsenal: "The reason I am involved in sport is to win. It's what it's all about. Everything else is a footnote." Kroenke owns several other sports teams, such as the Denver Nuggets (National Basketball Association), the Los Angeles Rams (National Football League), and the Colorado Avalanche (National Hockey League).

CELEBRATING ARSENAL

Since Arsenal moved to Emirates Stadium in 2006, changes have been made that celebrate the team. For example, in 2009, the club installed white seats on the lower level across from the entrance tunnel. These seats, along with red ones that make up most of the seats, create a pattern that looks like the team's famous cannon logo. A mural known as *The Spirit of Highbury* is displayed outside the stadium's south end. It shows every player who has ever worn the Arsenal jersey and team managers from the club's start through 2006. Other murals are located throughout the stadium, all showing special people and moments that shaped Arsenal's history. Additional features outside the stadium include statues of players and managers, like Thierry Henry, Dennis Bergkamp, Tony Adams, and Herbert Chapman.

In addition to statues, the club has renamed areas in and around Emirates Stadium to honor its history. For instance, the various seating sections around the field are referred to as East Stand, West Stand, North Bank, and Clock End, depending on where the section is located. Clock End refers to Arsenal's former home, Highbury, where a giant clock marked the south end of the field.

A bronze statue of iconic forward Thierry Henry celebrating sits just outside Emirates Stadium.

INTO THE FUTURE

Though Arsenal has faced many changes in leadership and ownership, it will continue to be a top English team. Arsenal's devoted fans will keep following their beloved Gunners all over the world. By embracing new leadership, working with youth teams, and remembering past glories, Arsenal will move into the future with hope and confidence. It will be exciting to see where the future takes them.

Fans seated at the Clock End of Emirates Stadium wave the Arsenal flag during a match against rivals Tottenham Hotspur.

CHRONOLOGY

1886 Workers at Woolwich Arsenal Armament form a team first called Dial Square and soon after renamed Royal Arsenal.

1888 Royal Arsenal moves from Plumstead Common to Manor Ground.

1893 The team changes its name to Woolwich Arsenal and applies to the Football League, joining EFL's Second Division.

1899 Harry Bradshaw becomes manager.

1903 The team is promoted to the First Division.

1910 The team is bought by a group of businessmen.

1912 The team moves down to Second Division.

1913 The team ground moves to Highbury.

1914 Woolwich Arsenal becomes The Arsenal, later just Arsenal.

1919 Arsenal is controversially promoted to the First Division. Leslie Knighton becomes the team's manager.

1925 Herbert Chapman is named manager.

1931 Arsenal wins the First Division for the first time.

1934 Herbert Chapman dies of pneumonia. Joe Shaw becomes temporary manager. Arsenal wins the league for the third time. George Allison becomes the new manager.

1939 World War II begins, and professional soccer is suspended. Nine Arsenal players are killed during the war. Highbury stadium is bombed.

1946 Professional soccer starts again after World War II.

1947 George Allison retires. Tom Whittaker takes over as manager.

1956 Tom Whittaker dies unexpectedly.

1962 Billy Wright is named manager.

1966 Bertie Mee is appointed manager.

1970 Arsenal wins the Inter-Cities Fairs Cup.

1971 Arsenal wins their first Double.

1976 Bertie Mee resigns and is replaced by Terry Neill.

1986 George Graham becomes manager.

1987 Arsenal wins the League Cup.

1988 Arsenal wins the Football League Centenary Trophy.

1994 Arsenal wins European Cup Winners' Cup.

1995 George Graham is fired for accepting an illegal payment from Rune Hauge.

1996 Arsène Wenger is hired as manager.

2005 Arsenal wins the FA Cup with a penalty shootout over Manchester United.

2006 Arsenal moves to Emirates Stadium and becomes the first London team ever to reach the UEFA Champions League final.

2017 Arsenal beats Chelsea to win the club's 13th FA Cup, a league record.

2018 Wenger leaves the club. Unai Emery becomes the head coach. Stan Kroenke becomes full owner of Arsenal.

GLOSSARY

acquire To gain or become part of.

card A part of a system used to discipline players during a soccer game. A yellow card is a warning, while a red card means a player is sent off the field. Two yellow cards equal a red card.

derby A competition between teams in the same city or in cities close to one another.

Double An achievement in soccer marked by victories in a country's top league as well as their main cup competition during the same season.

extra time In soccer, 30 minutes of additional playing time if two teams are tied in a major competition after the official time has ended.

forward A player near the front of a team's formation who tries to score goals for the team.

founder A starting member.

knockout competition Any contest where players or teams are out if they lose just once.

midfielder A player who is between defenders and forwards on the field.

pitch The ground soccer players play on.

plyometric Referring to athletic training that has moves that put muscles under stress during short periods of time, like jumping or skipping.

referee An official who keeps track of happenings on a field and is not part of any team.

shootout The process of players taking turns shooting goals until a tie is broken.

snub To reject or push aside.

sponsor A person or company that gives money to a team in exchange for its name or advertisement on a jersey or in a stadium.

stoppage time Time added at the end of each half as decided by a referee. Injuries or other time spent not playing can lead to stoppage time.

striker The player expected to score goals on a field; they are usually the last player to touch the ball before it crosses the goal-line.

table A system that ranks a team against others in the league based on each team's wins, losses, or ties.

tenure Time spent employed at a place.

winger A playing position meant to support offensive moves on the edge of play.

FURTHER INFORMATION

BOOKS

James, Josh, Mark Andrews, and Andy Kelly. *Arsenal: The Complete Record*. Liverpool, England, UK: DeCoubertin Books, 2018.

Lawrence, Amy. *The Wenger Revolution: Twenty Years of Arsenal*. New York, NY: Bloomsbury Sport, 2016.

WEBSITES

Arsenal Official Website

https://www.arsenal.com

Learn about Arsenal's history, current season, players, and news on their official soccer website.

***Mirror*: Arsenal FC**

https://www.mirror.co.uk/all-about/arsenal-fc

The UK newspaper the *Mirror* has its own Arsenal FC news webpage.

VIDEOS

15 Stunning Freekick Arsenal Goals

https://www.youtube.com/watch?v=TVROc24ykSY

This video shows Arsenal players completing difficult freekicks for the team.

25 More Famous & Emotional Arsenal Goals

https://www.youtube.com/watch?v=1zVfi3xiWEY

Watch a number of difficult goals by Arsenal players.

SELECTED BIBLIOGRAPHY

Auclair, Philippe. *Thierry Henry: Lonely at the Top: A Biography.* London, UK: Macmillan, 2012.

"Development Academy." asn.ussoccerda.com. Accessed December 2, 2019. http://arsn.ussoccerda.com/home.php.

Flynn, Alex, and Kevin Whitcher. *Arsenal: The Making of a Modern Superclub.* Surrey, UK: Vision Sports Publishing, 2016.

"Gooner News." Accessed November 22, 2019. https://goonernews.com.

Hodgetts, Rob. "Arsene Wegner to Leave Arsenal at End of the Season." CNN.com. April 20, 2018, https://www.cnn.com/2018/04/20/sport/arsenal-arsene-wenger-retire-spt/index.html.

Lawrence, Amy. *The Wegner Revolution: Twenty Years of Arsenal.* London, UK: Bloomsbury Publishing, 2016.

Lloyd-Williams, Andy. *Robin Van Persie: The Biography.* London, UK: John Blake, 2011.

"News." arsenalfc.com. Accessed December 15, 2019. https://www.arsenal.com.

Stay, Shane. *European Soccer Leagues 2019: Everything You Need to Know about the 2019/20 Season.* Aachen, Germany: Meyer & Meyer Sport, 2019.

Sunderland, Tom. "Report: Unai Emery to Be Named As Arsenal's Arsene Wenger Replacement as Manager." Bleacher Report. May 21, 2018, https://bleacherreport.com/articles/2777157-report-unai-emery-to-be-named-as-arsenals-arsene-wenger-replacement-as-manager.

INDEX

ABOUT THE AUTHOR

Joel Newsome is a writer and sports fan living in Massachusetts. He has written several other books about a variety of subjects from the history of the mythology of elves to the great military strategist Hannibal Barca.